USAIN BOLT

BY MATT SCHEFF

SportsZone

An Imprint of Abdo Publishing
abdopublishing.com

abdopublishing.com

Published by Abdo Publishing, a division of ABDO, PO Box 398166, Minneapolis, Minnesota 55439. Copyright © 2017 by Abdo Consulting Group, Inc. International copyrights reserved in all countries. No part of this book may be reproduced in any form without written permission from the publisher. SportsZone™ is a trademark and logo of Abdo Publishing.

Printed in the United States of America, North Mankato, Minnesota
102016
012017

Cover Photo: Yutaka/Aflo Co. Ltd./Alamy
Interior Photos: David Goldman/AP Images, 4-5; Jae C. Hong/AP Images, 6; Lee Jin-man/AP Images, 7, 28-29; Shutterstock Images, 8-9; Andy Lyons/Getty Images Sport/Getty Images, 10-11; Gouhier-Kempinaire/Cameleon/Abaca Press/Newscom, 12-13; Bill Kostroun/AP Images, 14-15; Oliver Multhaup/AP Images, 16; Anja Niedringhaus/AP Images, 17, 18-19; David J. Phillip/AP Images, 20, 21, 24-25, 27; Kyodo/AP Images, 22-23; Mark Baker/AP Images, 26

Editor: Chrös McDougall
Series Designer: Jake Nordby

Publisher's Cataloging-in-Publication Data

Names: Scheff, Matt, author.
Title: Usain Bolt / by Matt Scheff.
Description: Minneapolis, MN : Abdo Publishing, 2017. | Series: Olympic stars |
    Includes bibliographical references and index.
Identifiers: LCCN 2016951827 | ISBN 9781680785586 (lib. bdg.) |
    ISBN 9781680785869 (ebook)
Subjects: LCSH: Bolt, Usain, 1986- --Juvenile literature. | Track and field
    athletes--Jamaica--Biography--Juvenile literature. | Olympic athletes--
    Jamaica--Biography--Juvenile literature. | Olympic Games (31st : 2016 : Rio
    de Janeiro, Brazil)
Classification: DDC 796.42/092 [B]--dc23
LC record available at http://lccn.loc.gov/2016951827

CONTENTS

ANCHOR LEG

Only 100 meters separated 29-year-old Usain Bolt from history. The world's fastest man was in Rio de Janeiro, Brazil, in August 2016. It was Bolt's fourth Olympic Games. He had already won eight career Olympic gold medals. One more would tie him for the most in track-and-field history.

Bolt's final event was the 4×100-meter relay. His Jamaican teammates each ran their legs of the race. Jamaica, the United States, and Japan were all close to the lead. Jamaica's hopes came down to the team's anchor, Bolt.

Usain Bolt takes the baton to finish the 4×100-meter relay at the 2016 Olympics.

FAST FACT
The 2016 Olympics marked Bolt's "triple triple." He won gold in all three Olympic sprints in three straight Olympic Games.

Bolt runs away from the competition in the 4×100 relay.

Bolt took the team's baton and sprinted. With his long, powerful strides, he surged ahead of the other teams' anchors. The gap grew and grew. Bolt sailed across the finish line as camera flashes filled the stadium. The crowd went wild, cheering Bolt's amazing accomplishment.

"It's a brilliant feeling," Bolt said. "It's been a long road. I'm happy, but I'm relieved. It's great to be in the history books as one of the greatest. I'm proud of myself."

Jamaica's 4×100 team celebrates their gold medal.

RISING STAR

Usain St. Leo Bolt was born on August 21, 1986, in Sherwood Content, Jamaica. His parents, Wellesley and Jennifer, ran a small grocery store.

Sherwood Content is a small town on the island. Young Usain spent his days playing sports with his brother and sister. His early favorites included cricket and soccer.

"I didn't really think about anything other than sports," he later said.

FAST FACT

In soccer, Usain played mostly goalkeeper, midfielder, or defender.

Track and field is a popular sport in Jamaica.

Usain wins the 200-meter dash at the 2002 World Junior Championships.

It did not take long for Usain to turn his attention to track. Running is almost a way of life in the small Caribbean nation. Jamaica has produced some of the world's greatest sprinters.

Usain's interest in sprinting started in elementary school. But he did not become a force until 2002. The World Junior Championships that year were in Jamaica. More than 30,000 fans watched as Usain won the 200-meter dash. He was only 15 years old. That made him the youngest men's world junior champion in track-and-field history.

FAST FACT

At a junior meet, Usain got in trouble for a practical joke. He hid in the back of a van when he was supposed to be preparing to run.

As Usain got older, he grew to 6 feet 5 inches tall. He used his long legs to take huge strides. By 2003 Usain was one of track's rising stars.

Yet he was only concentrating on a single event, the 200. By 2007 he was eager to take on a new challenge. Usain asked his coaches to let him try the 100-meter dash. It was a good decision. Usain quickly mastered the shorter run. He earned two silver medals at the 2007 World Championships. One was in the 200-meter dash, and the other was in the 4×100-meter relay.

Usain, *center*, won his first World Championships medals in 2007.

FAST FACT

In April 2004, Usain set the 200-meter world junior record at 19.93 seconds. That time would have been good enough to win a silver medal at the 2004 Olympics.

THE FASTEST MAN

As Usain Bolt matured, he took his training more seriously. His fun-loving personality never disappeared. But he gained the focus that would help him become a track-and-field legend. In 2008 Bolt set a world record of 9.72 seconds in the 100-meter dash. It was perfect timing. The 2008 Olympic Games were coming up in Beijing, China.

Bolt sets a new 100-meter world record in 2008.

The gun sounded. Eight men took off sprinting down the track at the "Bird's Nest" stadium in Beijing. By the 50-meter mark, Bolt in lane three had taken the lead. With 20 meters left, he was all alone. Bolt appeared to ease up. He dropped his arms in celebration. He still crossed the finish line in 9.68 seconds. It was a new 100-meter world record!

Bolt easily wins the 100-meter dash at the 2008 Olympics.

Bolt won the 100-meter dash despite his shoe being untied.

FAST FACT
Beijing's famous Olympic track-and-field stadium got its nickname because it looks like a giant bird's nest.

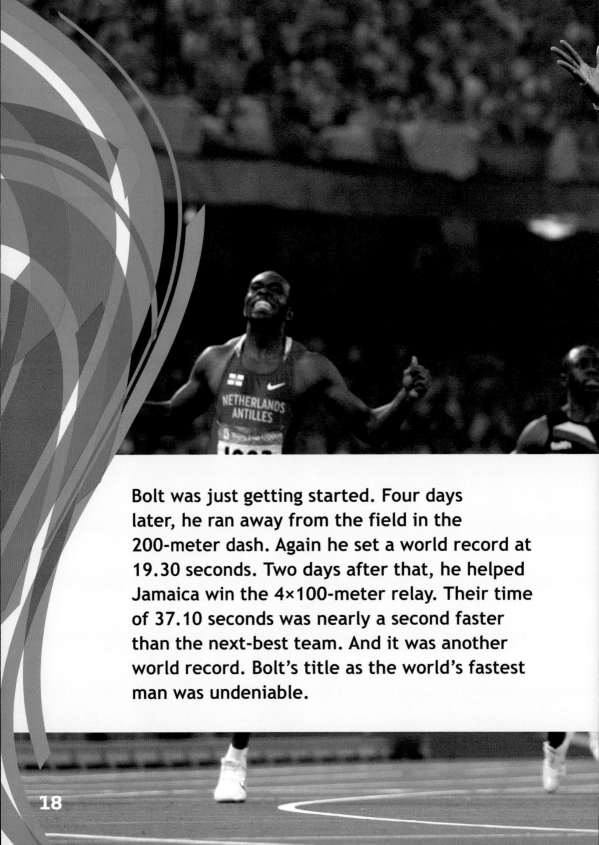

Bolt was just getting started. Four days later, he ran away from the field in the 200-meter dash. Again he set a world record at 19.30 seconds. Two days after that, he helped Jamaica win the 4×100-meter relay. Their time of 37.10 seconds was nearly a second faster than the next-best team. And it was another world record. Bolt's title as the world's fastest man was undeniable.

FAST FACT

Bolt became the fourth man to win all three sprint events in one Olympics. The others were Americans Jesse Owens (1936), Bobby Morrow (1956), and Carl Lewis (1984).

Bolt celebrates his Olympic win in the 200-meter dash.

Bolt at the 2009 World Championships

FAST FACT
Bolt did not defend his 100-meter world title in 2011. He was disqualified for a false start.

After Beijing, Bolt was the biggest star in track and field. His legend only grew. He won all three sprint events again at the 2009 World Championships. He broke his own world records in the 100 and 200. Jamaica's 4×100 time was the second-best ever.

Bolt kept winning. He won two more races at the 2011 World Championships. The stage was set for him to shine at the 2012 Olympics.

Bolt poses by a sign showing his new 200-meter world record at the 2009 World Championships.

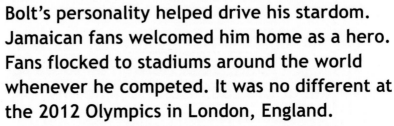

Bolt's personality helped drive his stardom. Jamaican fans welcomed him home as a hero. Fans flocked to stadiums around the world whenever he competed. It was no different at the 2012 Olympics in London, England.

Once again Bolt lived up to expectations. He won all three sprint races. No one had won those events at two Olympics in a row. Bolt set his sights on doing it again in 2016.

FAST FACT

Some runners appear very serious before a race. Not Bolt. He often dances and plays for the camera while being introduced.

Bolt celebrates winning the 200-meter dash at the 2012 Olympics.

FAST FACT
Bolt's fans love his victory pose, which he calls the Lightning Bolt.

LIVING LEGEND

Usain Bolt was 25 years old at the 2012 Olympics. He eyed one more trip to the Olympic Games. First, though, he continued to dominate in other meets. The 2013 World Championships were in Moscow, Russia. Bolt again won all three sprint events. He did so again at the 2015 World Championships back in Beijing. There was no question he was still the world's fastest man.

Bolt strikes his Lightning Bolt pose at the 2015 World Championships.

Bolt wins the 100-meter dash at the 2016 Olympics.

FAST FACT

Bolt easily won his 100-meter semifinal race in Rio de Janeiro. As he finished, he looked into the TV camera and smiled.

Troubling news soon spread around the world. Bolt had dropped out of Jamaica's 2016 Olympic trials. His leg was injured. Fans worried he might miss the Olympics. But Jamaica officials said Bolt could still make the team. He only needed to run well in another meet. And back on that London track, he did. Bolt was named to Jamaica's team.

A few weeks later, Bolt took the Olympic track in Rio de Janeiro. Once again he won all three sprint events.

Bolt, *right*, and Canada's Andre De Grasse smile as they finish a 200-meter heat at the 2016 Olympics.

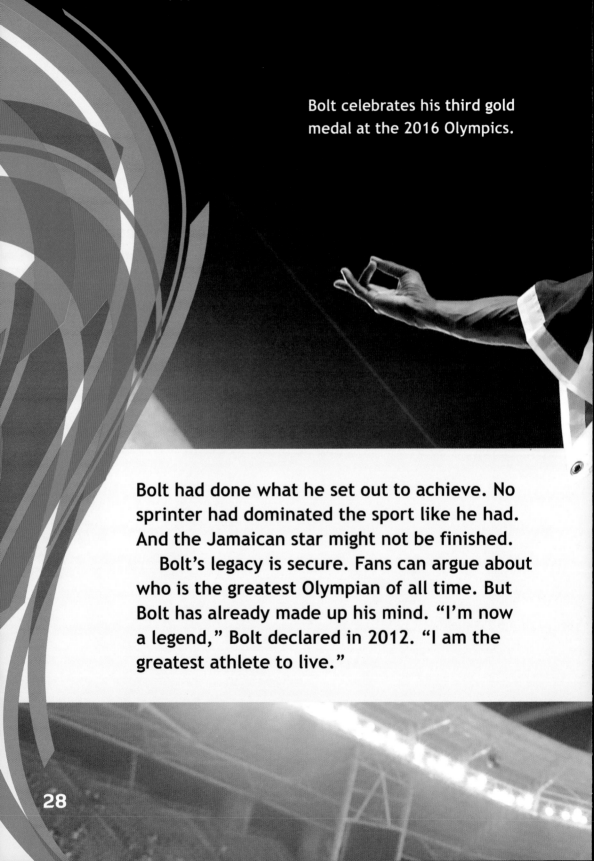

Bolt celebrates his third gold medal at the 2016 Olympics.

Bolt had done what he set out to achieve. No sprinter had dominated the sport like he had. And the Jamaican star might not be finished.

Bolt's legacy is secure. Fans can argue about who is the greatest Olympian of all time. But Bolt has already made up his mind. "I'm now a legend," Bolt declared in 2012. "I am the greatest athlete to live."

TIMELINE

1986

Usain St. Leo Bolt is born on August 21 in Sherwood Content, Jamaica.

2002

Bolt wins gold in the 200-meter dash at the World Junior Championships.

2004

Bolt makes his first Olympic team but struggles due to a leg injury.

2007

Bolt begins seriously training for the 100-meter dash.

2008

Bolt sets the world record in the 100-meter dash for the first time.

2008

Bolt completes "the triple" at the Olympics in Beijing, China, winning gold in the 100-, 200-, and 4×100-meter races.

2009

Bolt breaks his own world records in winning the 100- and 200-meter races at the World Championships. His team also wins the 4×100 relay.

2012

Bolt again completes the triple at the Olympic Games in London, England.

2016

Bolt completes the "triple triple" by winning gold in all three sprints for the third straight Olympic Games in Rio de Janeiro, Brazil.

GLOSSARY

anchor
The member of a relay team who goes last.

baton
A short stick that members of a relay team pass from one to another in a relay race.

cricket
A bat-and-ball game that shares some similarities with baseball.

false start
When a runner begins to move before the starting gun.

focus
The ability to concentrate on and work toward a specific goal.

junior
In track and field, a division for athletes age 19 and younger.

leg
A portion that one runner from each team covers in a relay race.

legacy
The accomplishments for which someone is remembered.

relay
A race in which a team of runners hand off a baton as they run legs in a race.

trials
An event that determines which athletes advance to a higher level of competition.

INDEX

About the Author

Matt Scheff is an artist and author living in Alaska. He enjoys mountain climbing, deep-sea fishing, and curling up with his two Siberian huskies to watch sports.